COMING OUT OF
MOAB

CASSANDRA L. MCCRAY

WESTBOW
PRESS®
A DIVISION OF THOMAS NELSON
& ZONDERVAN

WestBow Press books may be ordered through booksellers or by contacting:

WestBow Press
A Division of Thomas Nelson & Zondervan
1663 Liberty Drive
Bloomington, IN 47403
www.westbowpress.com
1 (866) 928-1240

KodakbyTee- Photographer
TranscendUnity- Designer

Scripture taken from the King James Version of the Bible.

Scripture taken from the New King James Version®. Copyright © 1982 by Thomas Nelson. Used by permission. All rights reserved.

ISBN: 978-1-9736-7315-6 (sc)
ISBN: 978-1-9736-7314-9 (e)

Print information available on the last page.

WestBow Press rev. date: 9/5/2019

Introduction

Coming Out of Moab

Book of Ruth

Many are familiar with the book of Ruth in the Holy Bible. "Coming Out of Moab" is based from the biblical context when Naomi and her family were in the region of Moab. Elimelech, her deceased husband had uprooted the family from Judah into Moab. There she would become a widow, motherless and face a famine in the land that was never fertile nor fruitful.

Naomi is described as a matriarch for her two (2) daughter in laws, Ruth and Orpah. These women were now in Moab as both widows and childless facing an economic crisis. Their providers (husbands) are now dead. Naomi is faced with losing the little family she has with Ruth and Orpah. She tells the ladies that she can no longer stay in Moab that she will return to her native land, Bethlehem. She tries to persuade them to go back to their fathers. Moab is Ruth and Orpah native land they are considered Moabite women. Here we see them preparing to leave the land, experience and even their culture.

As you read the book of Ruth along with this compilation of writings; it is my prayer that you are prepared and strengthened while you are going through your moabic experience. Please know this Litany of prayer. **You are Naomi**:
I Am Strong.
I am Resilient.
I am Anointed.
I am a wife.
I am a mother.
I am a matriarch.
I am a warrior.
I am a conqueror.
I am an overcomer.
I am equipped.
I am "Coming Out of Moab".

Your moabic experience may seem as if this famine will be forever but it is only for a moment. God places us in these regions to equip us for what he has for us when we enter Bethlehem (House of Bread).

I encourage and invite you to prepare your hearts and mind for what God is saying through these prophetic writings. I know that because He DID it for me, He WILL do it for you.

You are "Coming out of Moab", for many you conquered death, lies, illnesses, betrayals, failures, financial crises and other life altering moments- But you made it!

Attain My Spiritual Cap and Tassel

God is merciful, He is faithful to His Word. I know *"With God, all things are possible."* (Matthew 19:26, NKJV) I sincerely say that without the tone of a cliché scripture, but HIS words are real. The past month or so I have been battle tested regarding my faith, my character, my commitment to God's purpose that has been given to me. I realize that when we prepare for any test we go through a course, read the material, study the material, sometimes even do late night cram sessions, study groups with those that are sincerely focused and committed. As I studied independently, with a study group and even through web resources, I realized that the time spent preparing for this exam would not be easy. You see when we are at freshman level in this walk, we only get snippets of this whole course. As we progress through the terms and when we reach each higher level we are faced with different obstacles. But as Paul encourages us to stay the course, I will. Although, I am approaching the end of the course for not a certificate of completion but a degree that cannot be mounted on a wall, tassels, and cords that cannot be worn around my neck. But I will wear this robe which is my protection (the Body amour of Christ) and this cap which my Father in Heaven will turn my tassel and say, "Job well done my good and faithful servant." (Matthew 25:21a, NKJV) As I accept my crown of righteousness for exchange of the cap and tassel, I will just praise and glorify Him in His presence. For I have stayed the course, I've seen the promises of God and I know that WHEN this world comes to an end and I am in the New Jerusalem, I can find sweet rest in my Father's arms. Then I can say hello to my natural father and let him know how many days I wanted to hear his voice but God in Heaven kept me, when I needed my Daddy to cry to that God provided me this altar to bear all my burdens on. When I needed Him to be a resource for his little baby girl that Jesus had already paid the price and my ransom for my redemption. So, I would only need to really say, "Wait, I love you" and just smile. You see I am not looking for cum laude, summa cum laude nor magna cum laude but YES, MY LORDYYY!! I HAVE ATTAINED!!!

Immeasurable Blessings

We serve an unlimited God! Stop putting limits on your blessings…receive it running over and shaken together. We pray humbly for some things BUT He is a radical God. You cannot even receive it all. That is a promise He made! Be Blessed!

In Luke 6:38 NKJV, Christ tells us *"Give, and it will be given to you; good measure, pressed down, shaken together, and running over will be put into your bosom. For with the same measure that you use, it will be measured back to you."*

In Malachi 3:10 NKJV, the Lord of hosts says "Bring all the tithes into the storehouse, that there may be food in My house, and try Me now in this; If I will not open for you the windows of heaven and pour out for you such blessing that there will not be room enough to receive it."

Become More Than a Cliché

Many times, we hear Bible verses recited, made into a form of wall or desk deco, embossed on leather journals, etc. I have decoration pieces, leather journals, my own personal favorite scripture but tonight I was taught and blessed by the man of God that we (churchgoers, Christians and many Bible scholars) have taken scripture out of context. Here are the two (2) that was shared with us.

"I can do all things through Christ who strengthens me." (Philippians 4:13, NKJV)
Here Apostle Paul is still in jail but expresses to the Church in verses 11-13 his contentment: "Not that I speak in regard to need, for I have learned in whatever state I am, to be content. I know how to be abased (humble), and I know how to abound. Everywhere and in all things, I have learned both to be full and to be hungry, both to abound and to suffer need." (Philippians 4:11-12, NKJV)

He has needs to be met while in bondage and the Church failed to bless the man of God. So, he relied on God! So now when you read, hear, recite, cliché scriptures you will know the depthness of Philippians 4:11-13, NKJV.

Secondly, Philippians 4:17-19 The giving and receiving:
Paul explains WHEN you bless the man of God; *"Not that I seek the gift, but I seek the fruit (your blessings) that abounds to your account."* (Philippians 4:17, NKJV) It will come back to you. When Paul was blessed with the sweet aroma of perfume from Epaphroditus, God was pleased. (Philippians 4:18, NKJV) *"Indeed, II have all and abound. I am full, having received from Epaphroditus the things **sent** from you, a sweet-smelling aroma, an acceptable sacrifice, well pleasing to God.* "Although Paul was full and lacked nothing, he wanted the Church to know that "MY GOD, shall supply all your need according to His riches in glory by Christ Jesus." (Philippians 4:19 NKJV) *"And my God shall supply all your need according to His riches in glory by Christ Jesus."*

It's like saying words in another language; not that you are fluent in the language, but you have been around the language long enough until you can manageably speak it. But you are only bi-functional; please study the Word, attend bible study and Sunday School where context is taught so you won't be cliché. I fully understand it now. Remember, I have the Paul like spirit. I SHALL ATTAIN.

Game Called Life

Although I'm not big on card games, I've been dealt a few serious hands of life. But kept my poker face on and knew when to hold and not fold. But for most of them, I had a full house, full spread, deuce of spades and racked up my chips and walked away a winner!

New Year, New Me

Another New Year's celebration! Although 2016 first half was a hard transition, from my illness in the latter 2015 to adapting to my deficiencies which the illness left, to having days of deep desires to get out that whole of deep depression and mental anguish until I learned what my assignment was; it's contingent to my healing. I will be given peace, rest, safety, comfort and strength. By the second half of 2016, I was ready to take on this given assignment, fulfill my purpose, started my blog encouraging the lost, finding Cassandra (me) after 40+ years of abuse, getting a more intimate relationship with My Lord, removing the things and people of the world from around me and within my circle. I took on the Paul like spirit that helped me press forward towards the mark. The latter part of the year the enemy was/is mad because once again he didn't take me out. Oh, he tried! He used people that I respected for many years to show themselves and who they value. As long as I am at that entry level, my spectators watched. Guess what, that was just a trailer, the full release is coming soon. So, keep watch my beloveds. Now that 2017 is here…I am already to ATTAIN!

Seriously, to those that thought failure was my destination my train never showed up…. I didn't get left, I decided to fly instead. To those that still know my talents, gifts and believe in my purpose; you will be mentioned in my acceptance speech and the awards ceremony for Best Book of 2017 cited by the NY Times!!

The Lord has just begun. Remember, to those that chose to hurt me, continue to kick me while I was down, plotted against me, talked about me, stole from me, attacked my character, integrity and my family; thank you for pushing me to not just know God but seek Him daily. You too shall be healed. Happy New Year's God's people.

Thankful and Glorifying

Laughing at you Devil…it did not work. When you are committed to the glorification of God and not to self it will work. As I was told, "All closed eyes aren't sleep and all closed mouths aren't mute." So, I still say Happy Thanksgiving! I am still praising Him even through this mess you tried to create when you threw the rock and hid your hand… My vision is not limited to just me; God has given me a vision of great magnitude.

Vision Requires Light

Vision…. allows me to see many opportunities that lie ahead but it's so blinding to those that are not visionaries themselves. See light has to enter the eye so that I can truly see. My Christ is my light and salvation.

Fathers Do Matter!

Today, is Father's Day. So many have transcended to Heaven and many are still amongst us. I recently became a glam-mother again, a handsome little boy.

I think about the birth of a child when a mother is in labor, but I also think about the fathers regardless of the circumstances. The emotions are felt when a man has a son and gives him his name to carry on the legacy or when a father holds his daughter for the first time and tears begins to full up the wells of his eyes; are moments that are priceless. "Fathers do Matter!" In today's sermon it was said that until you get the Word in your heart only then will you be a great father. Fathers set the standard of his household. Joshua said, "But as for me and my house, we will serve the Lord." (Joshua 24:15d NKJV)

The Command Center Under Attack

We must understand our gift of service. We have been entrusted by God to help His people rather through products or services. Remember and do not take for granted what your assignment is. You must understand it's not about YOU. When opposition, no support, haters, nay-sayers come for you, JUST STAND! This battle is a spiritual war that the enemy has enacted to steal, kill and destroy. Your heart belongs to God so the next thing the enemy will attack is your mind. His mission is to take the command center of your being and destroy it. You see, he knows if he can get your mind all else will be under attack i. e. finances, relationships, decision making. I say this to all that reads this, we have already won this battle just buckle down and praise your way through.

He is the Only Gift

It's Christmas! Thank God for this new day of grace and mercy. But a special thanks for Emmanuel, the Prince of Peace, the Messiah, Sweet Baby Jesus, King of Kings.

Although, last night's travel to the inn that was occupied with no vacancies does not leave us with a room. Even though, our baby was birthed in a stable. He led us into a place of safety that was covered and prepared. Although, we placed him in a manger, we had some where to rest and be taken care of so that we can be received. Although, the wise men persistently seek when the King was born, God provided a North Star as a light in the midnight travels, you see He is there with us, for He is a light upon my feet. Although, Mary bore the true pain of delivery, she knew it was worth it all. You see she is the only Mother in creation that has seen her son born twice. (You will get it later) Although, we may not have gotten all on the list. Jesus is enough; Amazon Prime can't ship Him to you in 2 days, FedEx and UPS can't leave Him on your porch without a signature and USPS don't have enough stamps to cover His arrival. So, seek Him, praise Him, kneel down before Him and honor our Living King.

Giving Thanks Even During Your Darkest Night

Happy Thanksgiving! I pray that each of you had a festive day with your love ones. I ask that you reach out to someone that may need a word of reassurance. Although, today may look gloomy due to losing a loved one, just let them know that joy truly does comes in the morning. The darkest part of the night is just before dawn. Oh, but when the sun rise, you will receive that joy that has healing power. I love each one of you rather we know each other through an acquaintance or God's intent.

A Mother's Joy

Happy Mother's Day! Did you know that Mary is the only Mother that saw her child born twice? Hallelujah!!!! Conceived by the Spirit, Baptized in the water and spirit, Crucified on the Cross, Buried in a borrowed tomb, Resurrected from death and is the Living King.

Why?

My Why!

Because….

How much?

All I have…

Regrets?

No…I've been redeemed from things of the past.

What's next?

Living my purpose fully!!!

How much will it cost?

My life…

Have you prepared?

It was predestined before conception….

How will you know?

Because of my passion, my healing, my journey, my tears, my fears are not under my control any more.

Can I get this in writing?

Yes, read your bible!!!

A Crossing Path

Last night I spoke with a young lady that I've known for a few years now. I always admired how she carried herself especially being an entrepreneur. She blessed my spirit more than she will ever know. She must realize that she has a specific calling on her life. Many times, we meet people not knowing what struggles in life they may have endured. Now you meet them in the victorious state. When God has conquered and defeated the enemy on your behalf. The enemy knew that God had predestined her with prosperity, success and the opportunity to be among people of richness and wealth. I say this "Thank you", many times I feel alone in this journey, but I know God is with me. But my daily struggles make me feel as if "I'm alone." Although I do not allow the enemy to speak into my spirit; I just think that my next breath from these panic attacks may be my last or this one is of such a magnitude that the little oil I have left in my vessel will evaporate. You can never look at a person and tell what their story is, especially whenever you see them, they are always smiling and open to give to others. As I type this, I am so happy about what is to come in this woman's life. Stand strong my sister, stay in the race and have a Paul-like spirit of regardless "God got this." You know who you are and know that I love you. Paths are made for you to follow but along the path you meet a person that is on the same journey as you. That's called God's ordered steps and intentionality.

Oh, to be Kept!

I've stood among 1500 men or more during my 20-year tenure with the Florida Department of Corrections. They trained us, they also said, "the day you walk in those gates and the hair doesn't stand up on the back of your neck; is the day you shouldn't come back!" That was inbreeded into us! But since I never had hair on the back of my neck. I relied on my faith, my God and His words of Psalm 23. Oh, yes there were some moments that I was prepared for whatever, through the training. But scared, fearful or frighten never I. You see God kept me from all harm and dangers; seen and unseen. Whatever you may fear rather it is physical, financial or whatever it may be. Know this GOD IS A KEEPER!!

Morning Manna

I just wanted to share some morning manna. Enjoy, the word of the Lord it will sustain you even your hunger and thirst. Be blessed!!!

Winning is not always finishing first; sometimes winning is just finishing. We will not be remembered by how well we began but by how well we finish.

Colossians 3:23 (NKJV) says, "And whatever you do, do it heartily, as to the Lord and not the men." II Timothy 4:7 (NKJV) says, "I have fought the good fight, I have finished the race, I have kept the faith."

This race is not over, we been given a deadline but that is just a benchmark so that God will show himself a proof. One of my dearest colleagues stated to me "I am not dead yet!" Although he says things in a jokingly manner, but this is REAL. So, don't give up and don't give in! If you feel like you got to burn the candle at both ends to get it done; remember this *Little Faith, Little Power, Great Faith, Great Power!* To understand God's intent and His will; you must spend time with Him, reading His word, asking for clarity and understanding. He will open hearts, minds, eyes and ears to hear His voice. Wait on Him, listen for His voice and spend that time seeking Him daily.

A Prayer

Now I lay me down to sleep,
I pray to the Lord my soul to keep.
And if I should die before I wake,
just know I did it for God's sake.

As I continue to pray, I thank Him for this day.
I can truly say, that he made a way.

Although trials came from near and far,
All I know is "Jesus You Are!"
As my weary body begin to rest,
I know this storm is simply a test.

So, as I continue to look towards the hill which cometh my help,
I can sleep in a heavenly rest. Amen.

Hurt People, Hurt People!

Just some love from me to you during this day the Lord has made, and we SHALL rejoice and be glad in it. Many times, we go through life not really understanding the true meaning and actions of these words: hurt, pain, selfishness, egoistic, and so many others that are not of God. They are contrary to His spirit and His will. I own a t-shirt that reads "Hurt People, Hurt People". (Pause and really take it in).

We as followers of Christ should remind ourselves daily of the "Fruits of the Spirit" and also that there are many in this world that is HURT! You can see because of generational curses, generational pains that were never treated they were passed on to others by HURT through alcoholism, sexual abuse, physical abuse, verbal abuse, drug use, authoritarian behaviors, human trafficking, narcissist leadership, and so much more.

So, when Hurt People, Hurt People, it is a cry out to God. A plea for his mercies, forgiveness, deliverance, and most of all teach us agape love.

Labels are Stickers

As a parent you never want your child to be sick; rather it's a cold, fever or any of the critical or chronic illnesses. Yesterday, I was diagnosed with Adult ADHD. (Attention Deficient Hyperactivity Disorder) You would think that at my age this would be kind of strange, but it is real. My struggles have finally been defined and it finally makes sense to me. When my son was younger from the first grade up, he was diagnosed with ADD (Attention Deficient Disorder) I look back now, and I now understand what he struggles were like. See many people label ADD/ADHD within children as being defiant or just bad children. STOP THE STAGIMA!! I am not a victim of this disability, but I am an adult woman that need help chemically to focus. I researched the disability for adults more and it saddens me to learn just how much our babies do suffer when they are sick. I now realize that there are things and tools I will need to make my daily walk through this journey called life a little bit more manageable. I am still a survivor of it ALL!!

Get a Word

Take today as a planning day! Allow Philippians 3:12-14, NKJV to be your anchor for the year. Stop making New Year's resolutions that's so traditional and evident that its success rating is not very credible. As with any event or occasion, you must first brainstorm and determine your goals for this action plan. Allow yourself to go before God to allow Him to give you that ONE word. This single word will be your daily driving force to accomplish your goals for the year.

It is not as easy as you may think to acquire this word. First you must be sincere, you have to pray and ask God to give you this word. As I previously stated, it will be that driving force that only can be transpired by the Holy Spirit. When I first read about this 'word' approach was back in October. The writer shared how it changed her life in its entirety (spiritually, marriage, family and business) and I am now given my word. I shared it earlier.

Please don't take this as one of those random challenges. This will help you develop a deeper-rooted relationship with our Lord and then self. So, read this scripture, it will help you in the year from day to day. Take a daily approach instead of taking on big pieces that will overwhelm and discourage you.

Seek your word…. Philippians 3:12-14, NKJV
*"Not that I have already attained, or am already perfected; but I press on, that I may lay hold of that which Christ Jesus has also laid hold of me. Brethren, I do not count myself to have apprehended; but one thing **I do**, forgetting those things which are behind and reaching forward to those things which are ahead. I press toward the goal for the prize of the upward call of God in Christ Jesus."*

New Year Preparation

As the New Year vastly approaches, my prayer is 'if it's God will" for me to just see a moment, an hour or even a day! I thank you in advance. For many of us enter into our annual Daniel Fast. Yes!! We can be conditioning our mind, body and spirit man now. I am reading several resources to help me prepare for it and also while on it.

My areas of concentration are Faith, Fitness, Food, Focus, and Friends. (Anything and Anybody) If it's not to help me grow spiritually and to help support and genuinely pray for me as I take on new endeavors that will prosper because it is God's will. Shall be exempted like a school day, taxes and your Homestead Exemption. Gone…. but still loved!

You have to understand growth in the levels. As I reach a new benchmark, I have to change everything mentally, physically and spiritually. Everyone will not understand the next level. Many will support me while I am still at entry level but will despise me at an CEO level. God reveals all to let His people know who to be careful with.

So, if you can and will prepare as we take back what we lost in the 2016. As this Presidential Inauguration approaches, you will need to stay on a bending knee before God.

Double Portions

It's simply amazing how the Holy Spirit works within me. Saturday, I was listening to a TD Jakes' YouTube video sermon. His text came from St. John 1:14-18. (version unknown) This scripture is told by John the Baptist. He reveals to us several things.

1. The Word becomes flesh, here you must understand John 1:1-2, NKJV (You have to read you bibles more, attend Sunday School, Wednesday night Bible Study and Sunday Morning Worship to follow me) *"In the beginning was the Word, and the Word was with God and the Word was God. He was in the beginning with God."* John 1:1-2, NKJV

So today, my beloved Pastor, Rev. Dr. Curtis Thomas was utilized by the Holy Spirit and brought me a second helping of this word. This story is do deep. It's so astonishing to know that in the Book of Isaiah, he tells us about the coming of the Son which is 700 years before Christ's birth. But the Word was from the inception of all things. So, when John tells us the Word becomes flesh, he's telling us how God (the Word) came into humanity (the flesh) to endure the same problems, and struggles as we do today. John witnessed so much of Christ's journey (John 1:15, NKJV) from the time of both of them being in their mothers' womb (Mary and Elizabeth) (Luke 1:39-41, NKJV) to his teachings, healings, his very own baptism and so many other great deeds in those 33 and half years. But to know that Jesus was here before he came (you missed you shouting moment) and (some of y'all still won't get it) let me show you.

See John 1:15,39-41, NKJV
"John bore witnessed of Him and cried out, saying, "This was He of whom I said, He who comes after me is preferred before me, for He was before me." Now Mary arose in those days and went into the hill country with haste, to a city of Judah, and entered the house of Zacharias and greeted Elizabeth. And it happened, when Elizabeth heard the greeting of Mary, that the babe leaped in her womb; and Elizabeth was filled with the Holy Spirit."

This is truly real, just to know that God-Jesus-The Holy Spirit is one. In order to get to God, you must go through Christ. The only way, you would be compelled to follow Christ is when the Holy Spirit enters you, sets you on fire, gives you that yearning desire for more of Him and less of self. Glory…O'Magnify His name!!!

God thank you for anchoring me in Your Word and ordering my steps to your chosen vessel Pastor Thomas for 15 great years. Thank you for your humbleness, teachings, chastisement, leadership, prayers, trust and most of all your commitment to God.

He can change your heart through your sight

O'thank you God! I am so full of your word this morning. I am so excited to share this message with you today. It is such a marvelous feeling when you experience a moment when your Pastor's teachings and your independent studies of the Word connects. O'Holy Spirit guide me with this! In last night's bible study, our lesson was on regards of helping and blessing others, being like-minded, having the same objectives and the same zeal as your leader. Rather it was a ministry leader or the Pastor. After the lesson, several members gave their praise report saying how since coming to Christ the "people" that they use to hang out with when they were "in the world" often make comments or sleek-talk regarding their "new life in Christ". They simply shared that they are constantly faced with these things. But they also said that they will continue to praise and worship God and even keep those people "2 Cadillac" spaces from them.

But where I am trying to take you is the story of Saul versus Paul. Most of you are familiar with this miraculous transformation. In the Book of Acts, Chapter 9 tells us that Saul was indeed a murderer and the scripture says that he was on his way and the Lord spoke to him and took his sight. (Acts 9-3-9, NKJV) So, as Saul made his way into the city (blind), the Lord spoke to Ananias to go and heal Saul. (Acts 9:10-12, NKJV) So, Ananias obeyed the Lord's instructions. Saul sight was regained by the scales falling from his eyes. (Acts 9:17-18 NKJV) Now that Saul can see, he now also knows that only the Lord has all power, restoration and forgiveness. So, Saul begins his journey telling the people about Christ. But because of his past, the people plotted to kill him instead of listening to what Christ had chosen him to do. Saul even had a witness to give testament to his testimony. (Barnabas)

Scripture references:
*"As he journeyed, he came near Damascus, and suddenly a light shone around him from heaven. Then he fell to the ground, and heard a voice saying to him, "**Saul, Saul, why are you persecuting Me?**" And he said, "Who are You, Lord? Then the Lord said, "**I am Jesus, whom you are persecuting. It is hard for you to kick against the goads.**" So, he, trembling and astonished, said, "Lord, what do You want me to do?" Then the Lord said to him, "**Arise and go into the city and you will be told what you must do.**" And the men who journeyed with him stood speechless, hearing a voice but seeing no one, Then Saul arose from the ground, and when his eyes were opened, he saw no one. But they led him by the hand and brought him into Damascus. And he was there three days without sight, and neither ate nor drank."* (Acts 9-3-9, NKJV)

*"Now there was a certain disciple at Damascus named Ananias; and to the Lord said in a vision, "**Ananias.**" And he said, "Here I am, Lord." So, the Lord said to him, "**Arise and go to the street called Straight, and inquire at the house of Judas, for one called Saul of Tar'sus, for behold he is praying. And in a vision, he has seen a man named Ananias coming in and putting his hand on him, so that he might receive his sight.**"* (Acts 9:10-12, NKJV)

This is where the Holy Spirit connected all of this to me. In Acts 9:15-16 NKJV, Christ says *"But the Lord said to him, "**Go, for he is a chosen vessel of Mine to bear My name before Gentiles, kings, and the children of Israel. For I will show him how many things he must suffer for My name's sake.**"*

"And Ananias went his way and entered the house; and laying his hands on him he said, "Brother Saul, the Lord Jesus, who appeared to you on the road as you came, has sent me that you may receive your sight and be filled with the Holy Spirit." "Immediately, there fell from his eyes something like scales, and he arose and was baptized." (Acts 9:17-18, NKJV)

Once Saul is transformed to Paul (Acts 13:9, NKJV), we now know Paul's commitment to Christ; in Philippians 1:21, NKJV. But here is the connection to your next flight. In Philippians 1:29, NKJV, Paul shares with the people that you must suffer things when you follow Christ. Glory to God…I just can't get over this great feeling when that touched my spirit. *"Then Saul, who also is called Paul, filled with the Holy Spirit looked intently at him."* (Acts 13:9, NKJV) *"For to you it has been granted on behalf of Christ not only to believe in Him, but also to suffer for His sake.* (Philippians 1:29, NKJV)

In closing, there is still time for a change in your life, for the scales to fall off! Christ spoke this very message to Saul and Paul reiterates it to the people of God. We must suffer to follow Christ. (Philippians 1:29, NKJV) I know we don't like to suffer from anything, but I have a Paul-like spirit. To live is Christ but to die is gain. Whether we live or die we will have Christ with us and in us. *"For to me, to live is Christ, and to die is gain."* (Philippians 1:21, NKJV)

I want to thank God for my Shepard, Rev. Dr. Curtis Thomas, if you truly want to hear what God says. I invite you personally to our bible study on Wednesday nights at 8:00pm. I pray that even one day it will be televised for my audience that do not live locally. That's what kind of vision I have!!!!

A Blessed Day on a Dark Day

Have you ever thought to yourself "God could've but He didn't?" I am sure that question has pondered through your mind once or twice throughout your life. As I type this commentary, I think of my times when God didn't when I thought He should have. But I know that one of the great mysteries of God is that Isaiah 55:8, NKJV tells us, *"For My thoughts are not like your thoughts, nor are your ways My ways."* and I look back from a career standpoint, I saw may others go to the next level in their careers. I am not saying that I am not grateful for my promotions and awards achieved. I am just brainstorming, I know that I hate to sound cliché, but I do understand "What God has for me, is for me." He has kept me from so many dangerous situations and so many times he just simply kept ME!

You know when you are going through the trials of life; we often begin to question his intent for our lives. I pray that each day, I continue to grow stronger in His will for my life and continue this desire to hunger for more of His Word and teachings. This Thanksgiving was different than the past 15 years, but it was still blessed. I consider myself very blessed to have step-sons, in-laws, nieces and nephews that respect and show me agape love. I do not take that for granted.

Gifts while you wait

Each time I write a commentary, my number one priority is to bless someone with a word of encouragement and let them know that our seasons are not for eternity. The Bible says we will go through trials and tribulations for a "little while" (1 Peter 5:10, NKJV) however meantime, you have to trust God and keep the Holy Spirit abound in you. Only He will be able to give you the peace that surpasses all understanding (Philippians 4:7, NKJV), the strength to carry on. Many people will say that when they came to Christ that they gave Him their life first. But through my studying of the Holy Spirit's seven (7) roles, He conducts in our lives. He must enter your heart and body and then you will be moved to give Christ your life. If you can remember the story of Ezekiel and the dry bones. Well it was the Holy Spirit that shook and rattled them to moving and it was THE Lord that brought those same bones back to humanity (resurrection); by even putting new skins on them. *"So, I prophesied as I was commanded; and as I prophesied, there was a noise, and suddenly a rattling; and the bones came together, bone to bone. Indeed, as I looked, the sinews and the flesh came upon them, and the skin covered them over; but there was no breath in them."* (Ezekiel 37:7-8, NKJV)

That's a rebirth, a renewal of your walk with Him. *"But may the God of all grace, who called us to His eternal glory by Christ Jesus after you have suffered a while, perfect, establish, strengthen, and settle you."* (1 Peter 5:10, NKJV) *"and the peace of God, which surpasses all understanding, will guard your hearts and minds through Christ Jesus."* (Philippians 4:7, NKJV)

If you are at a point of your life that your circumstances seem like those dry bones. I ask that you surrender your heart and the Holy Spirit to rest, rule and abide inside of you. (John 14:16, NKJV) He will be your comforter, He will empower you, He will regenerate you, He will guide you, He will unite you, so that you can Koinonia (fellowship) with other Christians; He will intercede on our behalf to the Father, *"Likewise the Spirit also helps in our weaknesses. For we do not know what we should pray for as we ought, but the Spirit Himself makes intercession for us with groanings which cannot be uttered."* (Romans 8:26, NKJV) *"And I will pray the Father AND He give you another Helper that He may abide with you forever."* (John 14:16, NKJV)

What a wonderful God we serve, He also gave us another wonderful gift; His only begotten Son- Christ Jesus.

Call on His Name

I was told there would be times that you would have to walk this journey alone. I did not realize that the journeys of others were according to God's will for them. As I take on this renewed life God has granted me, I walk in silence to see but more so to hear the chants of the negatives and nay-sayers. They chant loudly as though I can actually hear what is being said; but it's all a muffle to me. You see I have been on this journey longer than I actually realize. As I read and learn daily that God took what was meant to harm me and turned it in for my good. I envisioned the support of very few to keep it all honest. I always heard that your circle will need to change when you are going to the next level. The part I hate about that is "it's real". I pour myself into so many things and I pray that my wisdom and understanding of people and their indecisiveness would be casted out of their souls. So many want things to be about them when in the end God will get the glory. I pray for their wayward spirits.

I attended a webinar last night and it focused on the NOW and how we should take care of today and tomorrow will be already setup. Throughout it all I've learned to accept people for who they are and not expect them to be honest, loyal, faithful, supportive and even Christ-like. I've accepted them as they are because they have not fully surrendered their lives to God. They live as though HE is a sometime God, only when you need HIM. But let me share this with you, God is everything, everywhere, and all knowing. His names represent so much; EL Shaddai (Sufficient One), Jehovah Shalom (Lord is Peace), Jehovah Rapha (Lord who heals you), Jehovah Jireh (Lord who provides) and Jehovah Nissi (Lord is my banner). I could go on, but these are only a few names; I have provided a listing with many of His other names. But this I know; every knee shall bow, and every tongue shall confess. You will call on Him and regardless of our ways He will still answer. That's what good Father's do!!!

Your heart can be changed through your sight

Very few times will anyone see me without my glasses. A matter of fact I can remember my first pair. I was 10 years old; I was scared to let any of my friends see me wear them; back in the day you would surely be called "four eyes". I remember that morning when I got to school, I made my cousin wear them. I just couldn't! Fast forward a few years, when I had to do my eye exam for my restricted drivers' license, I failed. I can still hear the examiner say, "You need glasses, come back when you get some!" I was disappointed and shame. So as the years go by, I wear my glasses every day.

You see (literally), I had to face failure, disappointment and shame to appreciate the purpose of my glasses. Although, as a child I thought of them as an object that would bring ridicule, as a teenager I realized I needed this same thing to get me what I was trying to obtain. The eye exam was a part of the process. (You just missed your shouting moment) As an adult I love my glasses, I get to pick and choose my frames and more so purchased at a discounted price. (Glory)

I use my eyeglasses, not only to help correct my vision but to be able to see my way. You see, I wear transitional lenses, so when I change different lightings, my eyes refocus to the new light. (O'my God) As the songwriter says in the song *Amazing Grace*, "I once was blind but now I see", as Psalm 27:1, NKJV says, *"You are my light and my salvation"*, Psalm 119:18, NKJV says *"Open my eyes, that I may see the wondrous things from your law."* Psalm 119:105 says, *"Your word is a lamp to my feet and a light upon my pathway."* Thank you, God, you knew how blind I was and showed me mercy. You knew the path I chose to take was not your will for my life.

Reader, if you think that your way is dark, and you can't find your way. Take these scriptures as the first light which is the Word of God. Pray and ask the Holy Spirit to show you this light and revelation what was read.

His Promises of My Fruits

I am so full and rejoiceful this morning. First, for life its self and for whatever God blesses me or gives me, I know it's for my good. The lesson I studied this morning reignited some flames that were not out but were simmering. Let me share this with you:

"Abide in Me, and I in you. As the branch cannot bear fruit of itself, unless it abides in the vine, neither can you, unless you abide in Me. I am the vine; you are the branches. He who abides in Med, and I in him, bears much fruit; for without Me you can do nothing. If you abide in Me, and My words abide in you, you will ask what you desire, and it shall be done for you". (Ask and it shall be given) (Thank you Lord) *By this My Father is glorified, that you bear much fruit; so, you will be My disciples. You did not choose Me, but I chose you and appointed you that you should go and bear fruit, and that your fruit should remain, that whatever you ask the Father in My name He may give you."* (The promises of God) (John 15:4-5, 7-8, 16, NKJV)

I prayerfully hope this blesses you today. The Word let us know that were destined to be fruitful and abide in Christ. That's a big fruit basket!!!

You are a beautiful Poem

This your second piece of fruit. Many times, I am given the opportunity to speak about "Your craft versus Your gift" and I always use Tim Tebow's Story as the illustration to show relevance. This week in my devotional studies I am reading a series titled, "Shaken: Discover your true identity" (Tim Tebow, YouVersion Bible App) Look at God, only the Holy Spirit can bring such things as this so that it can be shared and let the people of God know how he is omnipresent!! So far, I've enjoyed it but today Tim stepped up and delivered me a blessing.

Let me share this with you: "Life is a Masterpiece" He references Paul by letting us know this. A man named Paul, one of the earliest church missionaries, wrote that we are God's "workmanship". The Greek word for "workmanship" is poiema or "poem". Think about this; before you were even born, God wrote a beautiful poem about your life. (Incerpt from Tim Tebow's devotional)

That is great news to know as a poem; where the words and verses flow. GLORY!! If you've ever read a poem and even the book of Psalm in the Bible, you would understand that the Word (God), the fulfillment (Christ), and the flow (Holy Spirit). #flowerty You are a beautiful written Poem!!

Today is our day for a 5k: My Race

Although, my take off was slow some days even a crawl but I knew God through it all. Some days my legs were weak and others I had to press my way through, I still knew that God wasn't through. As my course would take a turn, I had to learn that the Word of God was the prize I desired to earn. I could hear the crowd, yell and doubt. I just kept running and thinking to myself, they really don't know what this is about. I can see the "Finish" banner ahead, so I took a deep breathe to get ahead. I didn't look at none of the other runners, I remained focused for what was in my head. As this race comes to a close, I will not worry because God had blessed by soul. As it is written, *"the race is not given to the swift nor the strong but to the one who endureth to the end."* (Ecclesiastes 9:11 NKJV)

Although, this is a physical race, even at my pace I can see God's face. So now that I'm across the finish line; always remember that God is on time. So, encourage anyone that is in a race; yes, it is hard to see your own sweat and tears but remember we serve a God of NO FEAR!! So, take on the Paul-like spirit and obtain your goal so when you're standing over the finish line, they will recognize God still abides.

Please read the following, it renewed my strength, I even mounted up like an eagle and I am soaring in the high of the Holy Spirit.

"Not that I have already attained, or am already perfected; but I press on, that I may lay hold of that for which Christ Jesus has also laid hold of me. Brethren, I do not count myself to be apprehended; but one thing I do, forgetting those things which are behind and reaching forward to those things which are ahead, I press toward the goal for the prize of the upward call of God in Christ Jesus. Therefore, let us, as many as are mature, have this mind; and if in anything you think otherwise, God will reveal even this to you. Nevertheless, to the degree that we have already attained, let us walk by the same rule, let us be of the same mind." (Philippians 3:12-16 NKJV)

All in His Timing

Very few people know that I enjoy electronics from clocks to walkie-talkies. One of my favorite clocks is the Atomic Clock. If you ever had one or seen one its features are so cool. You don't have to reset the time, when the seasonal time changes is to be set one hour ahead or one hour back. This clock does it automatically. How does this tie into our every day businesses? Or Scripture?

Let me share this with you. You see timing is everything. When I stop resetting things myself without God's permission the time was always wrong. Even when I tried to close a business deal that would result in a big reward…it was delayed or denied. The atomic clock is a tool that is very instrumental in my life. When I thought time was up it was only postponed. Every time I wanted to give up, God reminded me to just trust in Him. I am able to say that, *"For with God nothing will be impossible!"* (Luke 1:37, NKJV) Time….is here…are you really ready for what He is about to do in your life?

From Failure to Joy

In my morning devotion and bible journaling, I read about the "FALL". Many have been through a FALL some time or another. We have a lot of American History, World History, and Black History that we can reflect back on to remind us of such times. For the social media generation, we know of two events: the 9/11 tragedy and the 2008 Crash of the Markets which affected every industry.

But in a spiritual text, a FALL, must happen. This at first made me read it again, then (praise break) the Holy Spirit reminded me of what Christ did for us! So, each lesson I am able to take what I've learned and not only share the word but apply it to my life. Because my FALL, is for purpose. It has brought me a mighty long way!! (You don't all agree at one time…lol) Because I am no longer ashamed to tell my story, no longer held by the bondage of fears (failure, loneliness). The Word allows me to be bold in all that I do to glorify God.

May these scriptures bless you as they blessed me!
"My brethren, count it all joy when you fall into various trials, knowing that the testing of your faith produces patience." (James 1:2-3, NKJV)

Our failures are not failures in the eyes of God. When we step out in faith, we always triumph, whether or not we are successful on our terms. Who knows how God might use our failures? Fear of failure can stop us in our tracks. But if we're not taking risks, then we are not living a life of faith, and *"But without faith it is impossible to please Him, for he who comes to God must believe that He is, and that He is a rewarder of those who diligently seek Him."*(Hebrews 11:6, NKJV) Playing it safe is no answer to the fear of failure; it will never satisfy.

Fearlessly Ready

I think about how God's grace has kept me. Even when I was in the state which I feared loneliness, failure, uncertainty of people, and circumstances. He kept me…He never left my side, he provided a place of refuge, a place where I can hear only His voice. A place not only gives me comfort but allows my mind and heart to seek His face daily. I desire to submit to His will so that His purpose for my life can begin intentionally. I always knew that "His rod and staff" comforts me but to know that I have a fullness of everything in the presence of my enemies makes me rejoice and be glad in it. (Psalm 23:4-5, NKJV) I have read, recited and heard Psalm 23 many times but now (praise break) I understand how David casted all his fears away in this psalm. You see the enemy thought that being with someone whether he or she is the God sent one or the one that wasn't but you went and got (You will get it later) was the one that you would have gave your last to but to only learn it was part of the enemy's plan to make you become dishearten, bitter, paranoid, suspicious, lack of trust, zero understanding, fifty questions but with no answers. You understand where I am going but (praise break) when you become relational not religious with God; you become fearless, you can step out on faith KNOWING, you can smile at the lions that told you it's impossible, they can't see how. But you walk away smiling on the outside, praising God on the inside and saying to yourself "they must don't know what MY GOD said" that *"With men this is impossible, but with God ALL things are possible."* (Matthew 19:26, NKJV)

So, if it's not meant to come to pass does not mean I fail to achieve my goals it simply mean that God is removing me from this place (the shift) and preparing me for the next level of elevation so that my praise can increase to the next level, my purpose will be carried out to the next level, my soul rejoices on the next level, my liquid prayers (tears) will cry out louder and more unto Him on the next level. I am ready, my Lord for what your word says. Cassandra shall do, not man. I love this…. breakthrough comes from my writing; my healing comes from sharing them. Glory to His name.

"Yea, though I walk through the valley of the shadow of death, I will fear no evil; For You are with me; Your rod and Your staff, they comfort me. You prepare a table before me in the presence of my enemies; You anoint my head with oil My cup runs over. (Psalm 23:4-5, NKJV)

Prayer starts at home

This week so far Nuriah and I have laughed, joked, fussed her butt out, went to meetings and mostly got stuck in the rain wherever we went. I just thank God for her, regardless of what I say, and she may not necessarily agree or understand. She still says, "Nana, I love you." I appreciate her selfless love.

I look at so many children in the South Florida region that may not have everything they want but I pray that the parents or guardians are doing as much as they can to provide. As the new school year approaches for our children take the time to pray daily with them, talk to them not yell at them. I sincerely want each child to have what is needed. God is our source parents, but He is also a provider of resources. *"Ask, and it will be given to you; seek, and ye shall find; knock, and it will be opened. "*(Matthew 7:7, NKJV)

Teach your child who God is; let them learn the Bible by sending them to Sunday School and/or Children Bible Study at a local church. There's no luck…it's called preparation meeting -opportunity. God's favor over our lives and a hedge of protection over our children and school faculty. Be safe, listen, learn and love.

When the route is recalibrated

Have you ever planned your career to be one thing but due to life circumstances your path changed? When I graduated from High School, I had been accepted to attend Gulf Coast Community College in Panama City, Florida. I had a roommate to share the expenses that was the plan…ok I was ready!!!

Due to my roommate's unplanned circumstances our plans immediately were halted and changed. I now was faced with a 'what now' look. I went to Basic Corrections provided by the Florida Department of Law Enforcement and then moved to the big city of Tampa, Florida at the age of 19.

So many people I've met along my journey, some I became great friends with and some not so much. Now that I am in the Finance Industry as my career, I am fully responsible for giving and providing above and beyond customer service. This is not a job it's my own finance ministry.

I think about the scripture John 3:16, how God "loved us so much that he gave us his only begotten son." What are you willing to sacrifice for the God that you proclaim you love? I can remember when my son was 4 years old and I had to leave him with my Mom so that my job could be started in Zephyrhills, Florida. I cried… now my son is 30 years old waiting on his son to be born… again I will cry. *"For God so loved the world that He gave His only begotten Son, that whoever believes in Him should not perish but have everlasting life."* (John 3:16, NKJV)

Readers *"Pray without ceasing"* (1 Thessalonians 5:17 NKJV) and know that God is our everything especially a comforter.

Never defeated but favored

"What God has for me it is for me" …as I sit and think, this song resonates in my head. I've never been a jealous or envy of others, type of person. I love to see people prosper; I love to see the underdog excel. I love when God shows up and shows out. I love when people think it's impossible to do something and God's word reminds us, **"With men this is possible, but with God ALL things are possible."** (Matthew 19:26, NKJV)

I know that each one of us may have started on this journey together but when you're anchored in the Word and God orders your steps the route changes for purpose. When you see others going in a new direction and they do not understand your journey the skeptics will say, "oh she/ he wasn't never going to make it anyways". I beg to differ; I believe that failure sets the stance for forward progression towards success.

God has allowed us each with new portions of grace and mercy daily. I am thankful. Don't look at others and say why she/he gets certain privileges and others don't just remember your journey is not their journey. Pray and press forward.

Growing Pains

I was thinking about at moment's notice your life could change for the good or for disparity. I may not have the knowledge of carpentry/construction; but I do know you must do the necessary work to get the foundation prepared and completed. What are we willing to put into ourselves to elevate to the next level? Not the level that you think you should be on but the deserving one…the sweat and tears of progression, the sacrifices and the giving of your time, your praise, and your volunteerism.

I think of Christ on the Cross; how huge the nails were used in His feet as they were crossed. The pain we as people endure is nothing comparable to Christ's pain. I do know that nails are used to keep boards/materials in place, but Christ didn't stay on the cross nor the borrowed tomb. This gives me hope that nails are only temporary. God will pull them out and give you the cement of salvation; His Word that will never faulter or change. Thank you, Lord, for your grace and mercy.

Stars, Gifts and Vases

I trust the journey God has commissioned me to take. As I travel, my day begins with giving reverence, acknowledgement, prayer, devotional studying and bible journaling. As I do understand it all now, that my struggles and challenges were for purpose so that I could hear God's instruction. Each day I am simply overtaken with the joy and peace that His Word brings to me.

When I thought very little of myself and my accomplishments during my storm, it brings a smile to my face to know that I am as special as a star in the night sky. In Isaiah 40:26, NKJV, it declares me to *"Lift up your eyes on high and see who has created these things, Who brings out their host by number; He call them all by name; by the greatness of His might and the strength of His power; Not one is missing."* This also fills my void of loneliness when I think no one cares or could imagine my daily struggles. I do not nor have I ever seek pity from anyone. I am a Surv-US!!

So today, as I do all days be thankful for this gift God gave me today called life. It's called a gift because we are in the present. For those that didn't get it…. turn to your neighbor and say "God is a gift-giver and it's not a special occasion!!" That's just how God does things. We could never gift ourselves a better or more perfect gift than the Gift of Life.

This month if it's God's will, I will have my birthday. If granted that day of life, I will do the same as I've done on previous days but with one new aspiration. Daily I will say these words, "Lord, here I am broken as a dropped vase which you made with your potter's hand. I ask that You pick me up and reshape me into a vessel that will glorify you in all that I do." Amen

Don't try me, I'm covered

Yesterday, was a day that God showed himself a proof once again. Glory, to His name, the only name that I praise and give my all to. The enemy is positioned in wait, but God has already won any battle for us.

I had faxed some documents to my doctor's office to be completed. So, in return I received a call from the doctor letting me know that I needed to sign a release form. So, I later provided his staff with a fax number. So, as I stroll around in Office Depot waiting for the Release Form. I called the doctor's office back to inquire about the fax bur to only be told that it will cost me $75.00 for the doctor to complete it. I immediately hit the roof; I asked the lady "are you kidding me?" "Just for two pages, I had completed one page myself and the only two pages were merely federal law citing." I was still hot, this caused me to have a panic attack right on the spot. So, I paid $2 for a one-page fax and left.

So, I was on the phone with my husband and he was talking me through the panic attack. God reminded me of a lady that I had spoken to about a week ago regarding this same lady at the doctor's office always trying to get money from me when I have a Health Reimbursement Account (HRA). So, I retrieved the telephone number from my call log. I explained to her what had taken place AGAIN. She told me she would check into it and call me back.

So, she called me to say that yes in fact it is a charge to have forms completed but (watch God), I had a $38 credit on my account and then she says wait (My God), your insurance company just sent in another payment to us now you have a credit of $118.00. My God, My God!!! My tears of frustration were immediately changed to tears of praise. WON'T HE DO IT?!

Readers just wait on God! You see, David in Psalm 13:1-2,4 NKJV, thought God had forgotten him, forsaken him, let his haters rejoice over him. But when we stop and remember that God is always there, "He will never leave us nor forsake us." Just let God be God…. Have a blessed day! It's already blessed!!

"How long, O Lord? Will You forget me forever? How long will You hide Your face from me? How long shall I take having sorrow in my heart daily? How long will my enemy be exalted over me? Lest my enemy say, "I have prevailed against him"; Lest those who trouble me rejoice when I am moved." (Psalm 13:1-2, 4, NKJV)

My Sisterhood is Strong

A few weeks ago, I posted a picture of a charm bracelet that I received from a nice lady that works at the Lexus dealership. It was amazing how God uses people as a messenger. That charm bracelet was a gift for her sister, but the spirit led her to gift it to me. (That's obedience)

This "Sister Always, Always There", inscribed on the charm; was my message that my sister in Christ, Dr. Tammie Madison-Howard would soon be transitioning to Heaven. At that moment I didn't realize it, I was so overwhelmed by the kind gesture and beautiful gift.

This has been painful and hard the past week, but I know that God continues to show me the understanding of her death. On the ride to the burial grounds I was thinking about Tammie and I last conversation Wednesday before she passed. I asked her, "Where would you like to have your business relocated to?" She answered, "the Richmond Heights/Perrine area." At that very moment it hit me like a ton of bricks that she was speaking about the Richmond Heights burial grounds. My God!! Thank you for allowing me to have a relationship with You that when You speak, I CAN hear your voice and understand that Your ways are not our ways. (That's relational and prophetic)

As tearful as I was during her Homegoing services, I consider it a privilege to have the opportunity to give my reflections of "How I knew Her." Until we meet again, Fruity keep flapping your wings and giving everyone that angelic smile. Love ya girl. Sleep in Heaven's Rest!

Rewards of a Leader

It takes a village to raise a child. In our days this adage was certainly for sure as a stop sign at the corner of a road. I love being a grandmother (NANA), although distance is a factor it's not a challenge though.

I made myself a commitment to become more community involved. I had the pleasure to attend a luncheon with YWCA of Miami. Other than a networking opportunity for me, it also granted me the chance to take my grand-daughter (Nuriah) to a college campus, have lunch in a formal setting, meet people in leadership roles, learn etiquette skills, meet and greet others politely and many other experiences but most of all learning; empowerment.

The organization had a raffle and we won!! At first, I was in shock, we went up to the platform to retrieve our prize. It was beautiful orange orchid. I was confirmed by God's presence in the room that I am where I suppose to be, and I am a winner already even before the race/competition begins. Thank you, Father.

I researched the meaning of an orange orchid and it stated that not only were orchids rare in the Victorian Era, but it further stated that it was a symbol of boldness, pride and enthusiasm. It was a perfect to give someone that is about to do something nerve-wrecking. I simply laughed when I read this because this is exactly my walk God has led me into. You see, faith gives me that boldness, the Holy Spirit allows me to rejoice and be glad in it. The something that God is about to do in my life will make the haters and naysayers think they are losing their minds. That's a praise break!!!

This is simply amazing that the meaning of the color orange aligned with the orchid's meaning. That's God…the color orange represents enthusiasm, fascination, happiness, creativity, determination, attraction, success, encouragement, and stimulation.

Confirmation…. I AM READY GOD!! I pray that this blessed someone that is about to give up. I was there also in that darkness, but God is a deliverer and a restorer.

Faux Diamonds

If I was an open mic and begin to tell my story of this love journey. I would be given a pill to get this out my head and veins. Because no one will believe me. I would be committed to a mental institution. Because no one will believe me. I would have been told that you really do not exist. My sobering tears is not just a mist. As the dealer shuffles the cards, the trump spade has landed hard. The kings of hearts never die but make a queen go to the side. I need my ace to blackjack you out. You see this card game is wearing me out. 21 is the perfect score…. I bust your butt on this poker floor. Baby, Baby I hear you chat…but yet and still it remains the same. November 17 I was free…. not captivate into bondage. I spit these words not to draw any kind of feelings you see. I just need you to be me for 2 or 3. Gosh, it's messed up as you can see…you would hide like a wolf in sheep's clothing. I write rather than cry. Especially when I feel that I am about to die. If you read this to the end, step up to the plate and take a swing. Sorry but you about to strike out. My friend.

Sleepless in Judah

My days and nights are never the same. Many days I see another new day without the opportunity to digress. From sunset to sunrise to sunset my lashes never blinked. Some say just go to sleep! If I could I would…I feel like a guardsman doing night watch, intaking every sound of the night fowls of the air to the sweet chirp chorus of the morning melodies.

O' great Jehovah, thank you for all that you are to and for me. Our Father, which art in Heaven, as I send up my praises to you; show thy face and hear my humble cry. For I am weak but Thy are strong. Your Word tells me, that the battle was not mine it belonged to You. You gave instructions to stand still; sing and praise. Then I realized the victory of the battle was in my praise.

"Do not be afraid nor dismayed because of this great multitude, for the battle is not yours, but God's. You will not need to fight in this battle. Position yourselves, stand still and see the salvation of the Lord, who is with you." (2 Chronicles 20:15,17, NKJV) *"Do not hide Your face from me; Do not turn Your servant away in anger; You have been my help; Do not leave me nor forsake me, O God of my salvation.* (Psalm 27:9, NKJV) **"In this manner, therefore, pray: Our Father in heaven, Hallowed be your name."** (Matthew 6:9, NKJV)

My obedience will not only slay the armies that comes up against me. But oh, the rewards will be bountiful, priceless, golden pieces, rubies, sapphires and diamonds. A reward and my hands did nothing but clap, my feet began to move in a praise dance. Now Lord, I can rest in your arms and know that I am hidden and protected from the enemies. Amen, Shalom

Who Am I…?

Hello World! My name is Truly C; all I ever wanted as to be happy and free. Throughout the years you see I couldn't be me! I was muzzled in elementary. To becoming a loud, overbearing and career chasing employee. After years of leaving a fight of 1000 souls, I set myself some realistic goals. Make them real and attainable they kept telling me! So, I as I reposition my pawn to make this next great move. I found myself wrapped up in everything wireless and tired. No one knows the dangers I've been through. Yet you keep looking at me; to only see that God knows what to do. I've ran, I've fought, I've been defeated and won one or two. But the feeling of me Living My Purpose Fully, can't compare to the feeling of liberty. See I am a new creation not a creature that writes creatively! As my pens strokes the paper, I look back and say, "Lord, I'm grateful!"
Written by Truly C
Chosen by Thee
Saved by He

My Shift Came

I hate the process of moving. You have so much to do. You see old memories of photos of your children when they were born up to their graduation. The stuff/junk that you accumulated through the years is unbelievable. You ask yourself "Did I really need that?" Yes, you begin to talk to yourself because this whole moving thing can be overwhelming.

We often hate change rather it's for the good, the need or the choice was not totally yours. Nevertheless, it is a shift. I remember in 7th grade I took a class about motion and how water can change from liquid to solid and vice versa. But I never really grasped the concept of how only God can make things "Change". You see as I pack my things, I realized that most of the stuff/junk was outdated, obsolete, worn, too little, too big, wrong style, wrong color, the list could go on.

All I know is that each day God grants us new grace and new mercy. For His grace is sufficient. My shift is here. I am stepping out on faith knowing that God will never leave me nor forsake me. I was in bondage for a season…. fear of loneliness, fear of failure, fear of self-disappointment, pleasing others, self-neglected, gave until I could give no more, and cried until my tears became invisible. *"And He said to me, "My grace is sufficient for you, for My strength is made perfect in weakness."* (2 Corinthians 12:9, NKJV)
"Let your conduct be without covetousness; be content with such things as you have. For He Himself has said, "I will never leave you nor forsake you." (Hebrews 13:5, NKJV)

My shift was real. I know my daily walk with God will lead me where I should be. So, I say to you, step out, step up, believe in God's purpose and know that *"With men this is impossible, but with God all things are possible."* (Matthew 19:26, NKJV)

Let the words of my mouth be acceptable

Sticks and stones may break your bones words will never hurt you. Many of us, use to sing this as a child not knowing it was a complete lie. Words do hurt…

The tongue is the most powerful muscle in our bodies. This muscle has so many features and tasks. We taste our food with it, we may even kiss with it, it protects us from choking or swallowing whole foods. But the tasks were manmade, the lying, the backbiting, the negativity that is spoken into the atmosphere but also the positives like complimenting, speaking this into existence as if they were. (that's faith) *"(as it is written, "I have made you a father of many nations") in the presence of Him whom he believed—God, who gives life to the dead and calls those things which do not exist as though they did."* (Romans 4:17, NKJV)

I've said things to people that I really didn't mean and some I actually meant what I said. But in the end, I felt remorseful. (That's humility) You see only God can have the voice over our lives, we must wait and hear Him.

A kind word to a stranger sometimes go further in meaning than to your own family. When I say I will do something or give something, I am woman of my word. It's taken me many years to learn to say I am sorry to those I hurt. But I realized that I couldn't ask God for peace and have malice in my heart.

Very few people knew about my illness last year. It was a time of healing, forgiving and accepting people for who they are and stop expecting them to be decent, Christ-like, professional, concern, genuine and most of all a friend.

Yes, words do hurt but it's the cowards that generally open their mouth and release all doubts that they are just stupid. Encourage yourself, speak joy, peace, love, faith, salvation, and kindness.

Is your bag weighing you down?

I admit that I love bags. I've been called the "bag lady". I love different computer bags from a rolling briefcase to a simple computer case. I love different lunch totes, non-traditional briefcases for business. But when it came to a purse, I am very picky. I always select a dark color i.e. black or blue of the Michael Kors Collection.

My purse really is heavy!! I have the usual stuff most ladies carry. With an extra wallet, business card holder, several other small leather Michael Kors purchases. I realized I was carrying too much stuff. As I look back the more, I was putting in my purse the burden down I became. I was restless, stressed, worn, fearful. Tested, broke and tired.

I ask you "What's in your purse, bag, or wallet?" The bag contains negativity, no growth, no prosperity, no relationship with God.

As I clean out the purse of mine. I am no longer purchasing from the Michael Kors Collection and whichever collection I go to will be filled with love, peace, forgiveness, kindness, faith, charity but most of all what God has for me (that's favor)!

What's in your purse? Have you really looked in it? Now is a good time to clean it out. Don't say you don't have some stuff in there because we all have sinned and fallen short. Let's go seeking not shopping for a new relationship with God and ourselves. No more baggage!!

What do You Do Now?

What do you do when you don't know what to do? You've reached a point of "What now" in your life. Those you thought had your back has seemed to be nowhere or no way to contact. You know those people…. your road dog, your ride or die, your back, your bae, your bap!!!

During my forty-something years God has granted me to see, I've endured a few hardships and struggles that confirmed the loyalty of people is as solid as a fresh puff of smoke. #not

I always want to bring a spiritual awareness in each writing so today; I think about the journeys of Christ. We have known many stories how he healed, restored, saved and delivered many. As I reflect in the natural how our journeys sometimes lead us to specific grounds that was certainly His will for us to be there. At this place we can be renewed and refresh. That's salvation!!!

I often wonder when Christ would go into the wilderness to fast and pray, when He would look down at the valleys that contained depression, loneliness, sickness, betrayal, the lost, the false prophets, etc. Did He just weep for us for a moment and then decide to do His miraculous deeds? I love the fact that we can cast all our worries upon Him. *"And when He fasted forty days and forty nights, afterward He was hungry."* (Matthew 4:2, NKJV) *"Cast your burden on the Lord, and He shall sustain you; He shall never permit the righteous to be moved."* (Psalm 55:22, NKJV) God specifically designed the human body not to be able to bare this cross, purposely. Again, just pray, fast, stand still and know that God WILL.

Seasons Change

How do you interpret seasons? We all know several stories in the Bible that were season specific i.e. the lady with the issue of blood. *"Now a woman, having a flow of blood for twelve years, who had spent all her livelihood on physicians and could not be healed by any."* (Luke 8:43, NKJV)

As I brainstorm about seasons, in the natural we experience four of them. Based on where you live you may see rainstorms, snow storms, tornadoes, hurricanes and earthquakes, etc. I've heard so many say "it's your season" when we are reaping the harvest. But when we are going through somethings, we say "I be glad when this storm is over." I've experienced personally both the season and the storm. I felt like the storm was going to take me out but (praise break) through it all I give God the praise.

You see your season is temporary, but your faithfulness is sustaining. These seasons are designed for purpose. Although, we don't understand in the beginning even while in it; we never questioned God's will. My storm is almost over, and this season too shall pass. Meanwhile, I know God for myself to be a healer, deliverer, restorer, provider, a comforter, and a friend. Face your seasons… remember rain helps flowers bloom and bring rainbows and sunshine (that's joy). Glory to God.

No Longer Easily Impressed

Should I be ashamed knowing things will remain the same? Smoked up! Choked Up! Ya you need to just grow up.

Wine me, dine me! Is nothing that I seek.... I press forward just because it's greater things for me.

"Fill me Up, Fill Me Up!" I hear the crowd roar.... but what they fail to understand; the reality is there is no more.

Drip drop, Drip drop! As the rain hits the window.... I'm riding down 95 as if I was insane!!

Cuffed up, Roughed up! Is the battle that we face... only to allow just enough space. That space that does not contain anything we can see, just know it use to be me.

So, as I take my seat, the smell of your past no longer captures me.

Knock, knock I hear at my door. I look through the peep hole and who do I see? Yea you guessed it.... It's G.O.D.

He says that when He knocks all shall be attained.... Again, my life is not the same.

Because this new me, that you see. Makes ya wonder "Hey what about me?"

From Bitter to Sweet

I kept sowing a seed to be, this tall tree that I could never see. The branches grew farther and farther from me. Now that this old tree is not what it used to be; it roots cannot be deepest as the sycamore tree.

For we know that a sycamore tree bares bitter fruit. It's taste alone causes you to regroup. The tree that bare the sweetest fruit, has now been classified the Jublieer. What fruit is that you ask? It's grown in a place that you are not. Its juice is sweet as nectar, I can't imagine just anyone picking that tree. The grounds are sacred yet not free. The hedge of protection keeps common folk from plunking a piece of this rare commodity. Written by Truly C.... Yes, that's Me! Mrs. Cassandra McCray to those that try to be.

2018 Mentionables

As this year comes to a close, I must let the world know just a few things:

1. God is faithful! Read His Word daily...

2. Develop a relationship with Him! So, when the enemy attacks you can call on the Jehovah of your need.

3. Develop a sisterhood of like-minded people that bring value and support to you and you offer the same. Time out for putting each other down. If you haven't experienced much in the journey called life; you are really fortunate, because some of us has seen darkness or at least we thought so.

4. Volunteerism is a recognizable service to God. Deflate your ego, pride, selfishness, boss behavior and instead give of yourself freely without being asked and thinking it's all about you, God gets ALL the glory at all times.

5. Mentorship is in demand drastically. Our children need really responsible, accountable adults that is willing to teach not preach to them. Most only want someone to hear them out. They may have an idea that's a paradigm shift, possibly they need someone to believe in them and can trust. This is not for just anybody.

6. Whether you believe that we are living in the New Testament and no longer under the law of Moses. Tithing and giving above what is required not only shows generosity but you may need those same offerings to help you or an immediate family member out. Churches are places of worship, fellowship and a place to bring your burdens to the altar and leave them. Not a check advance store, bank institution nor a savings and loan entity.

7. Be a blessing to your leader, Apostle, Bishop, Pastor. When you bless the Man of God and Women of Faith, you are actually pleasing God. He has sent His Chosen to teach, guide you, hold accountability for self and his flock.

8. Prayer lines are specifically conducted at different times for purpose. Develop one, join one, you will not always be required to lead but being before God at His throne with a new portion of grace and mercy is priceless. Allow Him to let the Holy Spirit be your voice.

9. Daily reading is another vital part. Not only is it refreshing but find a translation that you are comfortable and relatable with. King James Version can be challenging because many words are still in the Hebrew language in the Old Testament and Greek in the New Testament. Many like The Message Bible, it can be starter. I prefer the NKJV as you can see.

10. Fasting is a time of giving yourself wholly to God. Rather you participate in a corporate 21 day fast or do a 6am to 6pm water only; on nothing at all. There are many versions, but the important asset is that you will be reading the Word daily for strength, praying at a certain time of day in complete silence so that you can hear the still voice of God. What to eat? Based on dietary needs due to health reasons ask you leader for a prepared suggestive list. But generally, all natural, earthy foods, NO SWEETS, NO TREATS, NO MEATS!! The first few days will be a struggle, but Apostle Paul tells us *"I can do all things through Christ who strengthens me."* (Philippians 4:13, NKJV)

Things to do when you feel defeated

This also reminded me of God's grace!! Stay encouraged, focused, persistent, motivated, stay in the Word, dive deep in God's love. Whatever you do, Don't give up!! You got this Warriors!!! We are in the 3rd Quarter!

1. Read or listen to all of the Prophetic words that you have received,

2. Call the people who will PRAY for you not PREY on you.

3. Use the Word of God as a weapon. Weapons against spiritual warfare are Prayer, Fasting, Worship, Praise, and Testimony.

4. Worship yourself out of the situation. If you have to play worship music all day; create a playlist. Do it, just love God with all of your heart, mind, and soul.

5. Whatever it is? LET IT GO!! GIVE IT TO GOD!! LEAVE IT AT THE ALTAR!!!

We are moving forward not backwards. We are above and not beneath, Lenders and not borrowers, Owners not leasers, first and not last, We are always TRIUMPHANT!! *"And the Lord will make you the head and not the tail; you shall be above only, and not be beneath, if you heed the commandments of the Lord your God, which I command you today, and are careful to observe them."* (Deuteronomy 28:13, NKJV)

A Prophetic Shift

I saw a picture on a Facebook post, in the natural I see a lady walking fashionably in a winter setting. However, in the spirit realm God has given me a word to share with myself and you at this present hour. God's power is unlimited. He is literally shifting the universe for our good. You see in the photo her shadow proceeds her! (Glory) Whatever it is "It's turning around for me!" God is reversing everything prophetically…. the last shall be first, you are the lender not the borrower, you are the victor not the victim, you are whole not broken, you are fruitful not barren, you are hopeful not hopeless, you are healed not dying, you are restored not recycled, you are joyful not joyless, you are a change agent not an adversary of change. God reminds us to look up, reposition not just your feet but your mind and all else will be in alignment with HIM. Right now, you have been putting one foot before the other in your living and giving but God is about to Open the Heavens. Prepare for His Son's coming and your hearts to receive greater things. Your old moon season has expired; been passed over, overshadowed by the new moon. God is the Creator of all things, even the Universe. He has the power to tell the sun and moon when to cross paths, when the old moon and the new moon to pass by each other. This is transitions, shifts, manifestations, renewals and you are a part of this great day and movement. Do not take this lightly nor for social media sake. This is a greater message than a mere post. Accept It! Declare It! Decree It! Amen and Amen.

The Living Water has Power

Today was a day I truly experience the Glory of God and the Holy Spirit raising me higher and higher into the presence of God.

On 8/16/17, I watched this Facebook video of an Asian decent woman bathing, her baby. The process of how she bathes the little girl was unique due to her mannerism. First, she washed the crown of her hair with clear water, then shampooed and rinsed it out her hair. Then she prepares to wash her by removing her diaper; the mother took three washcloths and covered the child before placing her in the baby's bath tub. She placed one washcloth on the left side of the child, one on the right side of her and then on the third one in the middle to preserve privacy. The technique she used was that none of the washcloths crossed over to any other side of the body. The right cloth washed the right side of the body, the left cloth in the same manner as well as the central cloth. Each time she would use a washcloth, she would dip it or wash it out in the bathe water several times and replaced it back onto the baby's side which she was caring for. Once she completely washed her, she flipped her over with her head down, holding her in the palm of her hand. She began to rinse the child with the clean water that awaits in the second baby bathe tub. After viewing the video, I just simply thought that their culture of bathing babies was unique and how soothing the baby must have felt.

On 8/17/17, which is 8+(1+7) + (1+7) =24, I was driving, and three words came to me. Reveal, Release and Renew. After hearing God tell me these words, He reminded me of the video from last night.

This is the revelation He gave Me:

1. The water you bathe in should not be the water you rinse off with. You are now clean and restored.

2. The three washcloths represented the Trinity- The Father, The Son and The Holy Spirit.

3. The Rinse Water is the Living Water, each time she would dip her hand in a cuplike manner and pour it upon the baby until she was completely rinsed. Then taking a new towel and swaddling her to dress her.

This was a powerful revelation to me! I started crying out to God to "show me what this meant, teach me thy way and to give me the power to carry out His will in this particular task." Although I was driving, I was under the influence of His anointing. My heart was full, yet I was excited, I needed to share the revelation with some other like-minded. I called by sister's keeper, but she was still at work and the use of cell phones was impermissible. Then I called one of my Intercessory Prayer sisters to no avail. I kept scrolling through my Messenger App to someone that would fully understand what I was about to share. I shared what took place with her and she was so supportive, happy for me and gave me a few words of encouragement.

I share this with you let you know you have an assignment. Ask God to REVEAL it; Ask Him to RELEASE His anointing and RENEW your mind, your heart to receive this great RESTORATION.

NAMES OF GOD

ROOT NAME:	PRIMARY NAME:	DESCRIPTIVE:	SCRIPTURES:
EL		THE STRONG ONE	
	SHADDAI	ALL SUFFICIENT	GENESIS 17:1, 35:11, 48:3, 49:25
		GOD ALMIGHTY	PSALM 91:1
	ELYON	GOD MOST HIGH	GENESIS 14:18
			PSALM 7:17 PS. 78:35
			ACTS 16:17
	ROI	THE GOD WHO SEES	GENESIS 16:13
	OLAM	THE EVERLASTING GOD	PSALM 90:2
		THE ETERNAL GOD	ISAIAH 40:28 ROMANS 1:20
		THE UNCHANGING	MALACHI 3:6
	HANE'EMAN	THE FAITHFUL GOD	DEUTRONOMY 7:9
	HAGADOL	THE GREAT GOD	DEUTRONOMY 10:17
	HAKADOSH	THE HOLY GOD	ISAIAH 5:16
	YISRAEL	THE GOD OF ISRAEL	PSALM 68:35
	HASHAMAYIM	GOD OF THE HEAVENS	PSALM 136:26
	DE'OT	THE GOD OF KNOWLEDGE	1 SAMUEL 2:3
	EMET	THE GOD OF TRUTH	PSALM 31:5
	YESHUATI	THE GOD OF MY SALVATION	ISAIAH 12:2
	IMMANUEL	GOD IS WITH US (I AM)	ISAIAH 7:14 8:8,10
	ECHAD	THE ONE GOD	MALACHI 2:10
	ELOHE		GENESIS 33:20
	ELAH		
	YERUSH'LEM	GOD OF JERUSALEM	EZRA 7:19
	SH'MAYA	GOD OF HEAVEN	EZRA 7:23
	SH'MAYA V'ARAH	GOD OF HEAVEN AND EARTH	EZRA 5:11
	YISRAEL	GOD OF ISRAEL	EZRA 5:1
*INTERCHANGABLE	ELOHIM	GOD THE CREATOR	GENESIS 1:1
	ELOHAY	GOD OF GODS	DEUTRONOMY 10:17
	MIKAROV	GOD WHO IS NEAR	JEREMIAH 23:23
	MAUZI	GOD OF MY STRENGTH	PSALM 43:2 HABAKKUK 3:19

ROOT NAME:	PRIMARY NAME:	DESCRIPTIVE:	SCRIPTURES:
	KEDEM	GOD OF THE BEGINNING	DEUTRONOMY 33:27
	MISHPAT	GOD OF JUSTICE	ISAIAH 30:18
	SELICHOT	GOD OF FORGIVENESS	NEHEMIAH 9:17
	MAROM	GOD OF HEIGHTS	MICAH 6:6
	TEHILATI	GOD OF MY PRAISE	PSALM 109:1
	YISHI	GOD OF MY SALVATION	PSALM 18:46
	KEDOSHIM	HOLY GOD	LEVITICUS 19:2 JOSHUA 24:19
	CHAIYIM	LIVING GOD	JEREMIAH 10:10
ABBA		FATHER	GALATIANS 4:6 ROMANS 8:15
ADONAI		THE GOD WHO IS IN CHARGE	EZEKIEL 16:8
		THE LORD	
		MY GREAT LORD	
YAH		I AM, THE ONE WHO IS	EXODUS 15:2 PSALM 68:4
		THE SELF EXISTENT ONE	ISAIAH 26:4
YHWH		GOD WHO IS ALWAYS THERE	EXODUS 3:13-14
*INTERCHANGABLE			
YAHWEH	JEHOVAH	LORD (I AM)	EXODUS 3:13-14, 6:2-3
YIREH	JIREH	THE LORD WILL PROVIDE	GENESIS 22:14 PSALM 23:1
	NISSI	THE LORD IS MY BANNER	EXODUS 17:15 ISAIAH 11:12
			DEUTRONOMY 20:3-4
			EPHESIANS 6:10-18
	RAPHA	THE LORD WHO HEALS YOU	EXODUS 15:26 PSALM 103:3
			1 PETER 2:24 PSALM 147:3
	SHALOM	THE LORD IS PEACE	NUMBERS 6:22-27
			JUDGES 6:24 ISAIAH 9:6
			HEBREWS 13:20

ROOT NAME:	PRIMARY NAME:	DESCRIPTIVE:	SCRIPTURES:
	MEKADDISHKEM	THE LORD WHO SANCTIFIES	EXODUS 31:12-13
			1 THESSOLONIANS 5:23
	ROHI	THE LORD IS MY SHEPHERD	PSALM 1 JOHN 10:14-16
			HEBREWS 13:20 ROMANS 9:29
	SHAMMAH	THE LORD IS THERE	EZRA 48:35
		THE LORD IS MY COMPANION	MATTHEW 28:20
			REVELATION 21:3
	TSIDKENU	THE LORD OUR RIGHTEOUSNESS	JEREMIAH 23:5-6, 33:16
			2 CORINTHIANS 5:21

Reference:
https://www.allaboutgod.com

About Author

Ms. Cassandra McCray is a native of Florida born and raised. She is a mother of two (2) and two (2) grandchildren. She has a broad background in Financial Services and Criminal Justice. After working nearly 20 years for the Florida Department Corrections throughout the State of Florida, she transitioned into the finance industry. Cassandra is very passionate about teaching others how to protect and prepare for the future both in earthly realm and supernaturally. In May 2016, Cassandra heard the voice of God and His instructions. She heeded to His voice and obeyed. During this time Cassandra began to become introduced to her God given prophetic gift as a scriber; her non-profit organization, Living My Purpose Fully, Inc. was instituted, and she immediately began to write.

Due to season of preparation, God placed several books in her belly and brought forth an opportunity to moderate an online prayer ministry. Initially, We_Pray1 Global Ministries was established and was broadcasted on several platforms. In December 2018, after much prayer, fasting and supplication; the ministry was reorganized and came in alignment with doctrine. The Ministry now known as G.I.F.T.S. Outreach, believes that we have grace, intercession, faith, talents and salvation as gifts from God as tools for us to assist in the building of the Kingdom of God.

Cassandra believes in the one Living God, The Risen King Christ Jesus and the Holy Spirit that dwells among us. She practices none of other that the Living Word; as a believer and follower of Christ. She belongs to the Covenant Missionary Baptist Church under the leadership of Rev. Dr. Curtis Thomas, Sr. Pastor/Teacher in Florida City, Florida. She is a member of the Intercessory Prayer Ministry as Tuesday and Wednesdays Lead Prayer Servant, an honorary member of the Board of Trustees and assistance the needs of the Pastor and the Body of Christ at large.

Cassandra is definitely a generational curse breaker, a lead magnet in her own right. She has won many awards in the Finance Industry, leads a global online ministry, written for two (2) newspaper companies as a religious commentary. Cassandra is the first African-American woman to write for one of the newspaper companies where demographically is just not heard of. She has participated in several writing contest and won the Jack Canfield Writing Contest in 2017. Her vision is to utilize her given gifts and talents to reach and teach the people of God that the enemy has planted lack in our mindset for generations, but we are heirs to the inheritance of Abraham.

Cassandra attended John Eckhardt's AP Global **PLAN, PURPOSE, and PURSUIT** ™ and the **Success Speaks Global**™ training to enhance her speaking opportunities both domestically and internationally. She knows that God is omnipresent and the importance of language diversity.

Anchored Butterfly™

Printed in the United States
By Bookmasters